$22.79

Shapes: Circles

Esther Sarfatti

Rourke
Publishing LLC
Vero Beach, Florida 32964

www.rourkepublishing.com

PHOTO CREDITS: © Kent Weakley: title page; © Jim Tardio: page 5; © Jose Manuel Gelpi Diaz: page 9; © Vasko Miokovic: page 15; © Kaycee Craig: page 17; © Jose Tejo: page 19; © Dana Bartekoske: page 21; © Renee Brady: page 23.

Editor: Robert Stengard-Olliges

Cover design by Nicola Stratford.

Library of Congress Cataloging-in-Publication Data

Sarfatti, Esther.
  Shapes : circles / Esther Sarfatti.
     p. cm. -- (Concepts)
  ISBN 978-1-60044-525-5 (Hardcover)
  ISBN 978-1-60044-666-5 (Softcover)
  1. Circle--Juvenile literature. 2. Shapes--Juvenile literature. I. Title.
   QA484.S26 2008
   516'.152--dc22
                                   2007014073

Printed in the USA

CG/CG

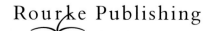

Rourke Publishing

www.rourkepublishing.com – rourke@rourkepublishing.com
Post Office Box 3328, Vero Beach, FL 32964

This is a circle.

Circles are everywhere.

5

These coins are circles.

This ball is a circle.

9

These candies are circles.

These wheels are circles.

13

These pizzas are circles.

These buttons are circles.

These flowers are circles.

These cookies are circles, too.

Circles are everywhere.
Can you find the circles?

23

Index

Further Reading

James, Christine. *Around the Park: A Book About Circles*. Picture Window Books, 2006.

Leake, Diyan. *Finding Shapes: Circles*. Heinemann, 2005.

Recommended Websites

www.enchantedlearning.com/themes/shapes.shtml

About the Author

Esther Sarfatti has worked with children's books for over 15 years as an editor and translator. This is her first series as an author. Born in Brooklyn, New York, and brought up in a trilingual home, Esther currently lives with her husband and son in Madrid, Spain.